WHITSUNDAYS

P E T E R   L I K

"My total dedication and obsession with
photography has taken me on journeys
into many remarkable areas throughout
Australia.
I captured this collection of images
using a specialist panoramic camera.
Because of the wider field of view, this
format enables me to portray the true
spirit of Australia on film. Upon viewing
these images I am sure you will share
with me the tranquillity and solitude
I experienced whilst exploring the
stunning beauty of this country."

peter lik PUBLISHING

PO Box 2529 Cairns Queensland 4870 Australia
Telephone: (07) 4053 9000 **Fax:** (07) 4032 1277
sales@peterlik.com.au   **www.peterlik.com**

© **Peter Lik Publishing**   BK23

ISBN 1 876 58512 9

Front cover - Aerial of Hill Inlet and Whitehaven Beach
Back cover - Whitehaven Beach
Additional Photography - Tourism Queensland, Bob Halstead,
                                         Murray Waite & Assoc, Shane Holzberger

WHITSUNDAYS

The Whitsunday group of islands are situated off the East Coast of Queensland between Mackay and Bowen. The islands are a mecca for tourists and their aquamarine waters and enchanting beaches have seen them become one of Australia's most popular destinations. In 1770 Captain James Cook sailed north up the Queensland coast and through the picturesque waterways of the Coral Sea. He passed through the passage on the day known as 'Whit Sunday' and so the name was created. Officially he named the surrounding islands the Cumberlands, but over time they have become universally known as the Whitsunday Islands. The group comprises over 70 continental islands, which are actually a semi-submerged mountain range once connected to the mainland. Changing sea levels at the end of the ice age claimed the surrounding landscape and now only the tips are visible rising from the ocean floor.

For those who visit the Whitsunday's, an infinite array of activities await. With an enviable tropical climate practically year round, visitor numbers to the area have steadily increased as its reputation as one of the world's great aquatic playgrounds has spread. From snorkelling, diving the reef and whale watching, to the freedom of bareboat yacht charters, or simply relaxing on one of the many pristine beaches there is something for everyone's taste and budget.

The Whitsunday passage offers superb sailing, and cruising the turquoise waterways on your own yacht charter is truly one of life's more pleasurable experiences. A popular stopping off point is the spectacular Whitehaven Beach. Its 6kms of pure white swirling silica sand, and sparkling azure waters consistently rank it as one of the world's best beaches.

Airlie Beach is the bustling resort town from which the Whitsunday Islands radiate and is the departure point for trips to the outer reef and islands. The main business centre of town along Shute Harbour Road is lined with cafes, pubs, hostels and countless tour operators offering day trips, dive courses and excursions to the reef. Though known as a backpacker's party town, Airlie caters for the more exclusive traveller as well, with superb five star accommodation and fine dining.

Seven islands in the group provide resort style facilities, and accommodation ranges from budget to luxury. Whether for a fun loving backpacker or a five star tourist, the Whitsunday's stunning scenery and laid back lifestyle makes it the ultimate tropical paradise.

THE WHITSUNDAYS - OUT OF THE BLUE

W H I T S U N D A Y

I S L A N D

Sculptural sand patterns created by the tide at spectacular Whitehaven beach.

Hamilton is the largest commercial island in the Whitsunday Group. Offering an array of watersports, restaurants, shops, nightclubs and even it's own church Hamilton Island has become a favourite venue for weddings and honeymoons.

I S L A N D

Whitehaven Beach is a popular mooring for bareboat yacht charters.

A sea plane skims the surface of Hardy's Lagoon.
overleaf: An aerial view encompassing the magnificent sweep of Whitehaven
Beach lapped by the warm waters of the Coral Sea.

Boats returning to Shute Harbour from a day at the reef.

View to Mandalay point from Airlie Beach.

A painted sky over Catseye Bay on Hamilton island.

Airlie's popular man made Lagoon.

Pioneer Bay Beach, Airlie.

Hayman is the most luxurious island resort on
The Great Barrier Reef. Offering exclusive five
star service and accommodation, it has been
rated one of the Top 10 Hotels in the World.

H A Y M A N

I S L A N D

The majority of the Whitsunday's are designated National Park and miles of established walking trails are a great opportunity to explore lush rainforests, or climb to one of the many lookouts and take in breathtaking 360 degree views.

opposite: An idyllic island hideaway.

Twilight falls over Hamilton Island and the twinkling lights of the Marina illuminate the harbour.

left: The sculptural sands of Hill Inlet snaking out to the Coral Sea.

right: The magnificent sight of a yacht under full sail cutting its way through the Whitsunday Passage.

From beachside bungalows on South Molle Island, you will awake to the sounds of the Coral Sea lapping your doorstep. The island is a paradise for those seeking fun and relaxation.

SOUTH MOLLE ISLAND

Hamilton Island basks in the warm
glow of a tropical sunset.

The recently refurbished resort on Daydream Island is set amidst lush tropical rainforests. A favourite island for families, it offers watersports, a large selection of restaurants and even an open air cinema.

The fragile ecosystem of the Great
Barrier Reef is home to more
than 1500 species of fish and over
400 types of coral.

It is the largest living structure on
earth, and is collectively formed by
more than 2000 individual reefs
ranging in size from one hectare to
more than 100 square kilometres.

The advent of high speed vessels
has seen the reef become more
accessible to tourists and it is no
longer the domain of experienced
divers or adventurers.

The P&O owned Brampton Island Resort offers a perfect escape to peace, privacy and relaxation. Lush National Park rainforest covers much of the 7.7 square km island and it is home to over 50 species of birds.

BRAMPTON ISLAND

left: Watersports on Daydream Island.

right: Yachts moored over the reef at Blue Pearl Bay on Hayman Island.

left: A pristine sand cay off Langford Island.

right: The underwater observatory at Hook Island. The island is also home to a wilderness lodge popular with budget conscious travellers.

Beachside bungalows at Peppers Palm Bay, Long Island.

Long Island is home to two resorts – the popular fun lover's Club Crocodile
and the more reclusive Peppers Palm Bay. The resorts are situated on
opposite sides of the island and divided by tranquil National Park rainforests.

Australia's own Club Med on Lindeman Island is dedicated to pleasure. There's always plenty to do on this international standard resort, or simply relax by the pool or on one of the beautiful beaches.

Panoramic views to Maher and Shaw Islands from Mt Oldfield lookout on Lindeman Island..

previous page: Every morning Abel Point Marina at the north end of Airlie, and Shute Harbour to the south, are a hive of activity as every water craft imaginable, from luxury pleasure cruisers to bareboat yachts, navigate the harbours.

left: Reef catamaran moored at Hardy Reef.

right: Relaxing on Hardy's reef.

left: Aerial view of Hamilton Island.

right: The incredible natural creation of Heart Reef.

overleaf: Paradise found on the unspoilt virgin
sands of Whitehaven Beach.

peter lik GALLERY

www.peterlik.com

Multi award-winning photographer Peter Lik proudly presents his
signature Galleries. The Galleries, with their handcrafted timber
floors and unique custom decor radiate a beautiful ambience.

The stunning 'Gallery Collection' is selected from Peter's library of
over 250,000 images and hand printed as limited edition
Ilfochrome photographs.

Entering a Peter Lik Gallery is a total sensory experience.
His connection with the heart and soul of the landscape is evident
and he captures the true feeling of the land like no other.

CAIRNS	NOOSA	PORT DOUGLAS	SYDNEY	LAHAINA	SAN FRANCISCO
4 Shields Street	9 Hastings Street	19 Macrossan Street	QVB, 455 George St	712 Front Street	Pier 39, Embarcadero
Tel (07) 4031 8177	Tel (07) 5474 8233	Tel (07) 4099 6050	Tel (02) 9269 0182	Tel (808) 661 6623	Tel (415) 765 7515

BOOKS BY PETER LIK

- Australia
- Blue Mountains
- Brisbane
- Byron Bay
- Cairns
- Daintree and Cape Tribulation
- Fraser Island
- Gold Coast
- Great Barrier Reef
- Port Douglas
- Sunshine Coast
- Sydney
- The Red Centre
- Townsville and Magnetic Island
- Whitsundays
- Wildlife
- World Heritage Rainforest

LARGE FORMAT PUBLICATIONS
- Australia - Images of a Timeless Land
- San Francisco
- Spirit of America

peter lik PUBLISHING